D0793153

MARINE MAMMALS
OF CALIFORNIA

BY
ROBERT T. ORR
Associate Director of the
California Academy of Sciences

Drawings by Jacqueline Schonewald
Photographs by the author unless otherwise specified

UNIVERSITY OF CALIFORNIA PRESS
BERKELEY · LOS ANGELES · LONDON

UNIVERSITY OF CALIFORNIA PRESS
BERKELEY AND LOS ANGELES, CALIFORNIA
UNIVERSITY OF CALIFORNIA PRESS, LTD.
LONDON, ENGLAND
© 1972, BY
THE REGENTS OF THE UNIVERSITY OF CALIFORNIA
ISBN 0-520-02077-4
LIBRARY OF CONGRESS CATALOG CARD NUMBER: 78-165233
PRINTED IN THE UNITED STATES OF AMERICA

234567890

CONTENTS

Cover picture: A Steller's sea lion harem.

INTRODUCTION

Although mammals originated on land from reptilian ancestors, several groups have become adapted to a marine or aquatic life. Those most specialized for life in water are the cetaceans (whales, porpoises, and dolphins), the pinnipeds (seals, sea lions, and walruses), and the sirenians (manatees, dugongs, and sea cows). A few species belonging to typically terrestrial mammalian groups have also become specialized for an aquatic existence—the beaver, muskrat, and nutria among rodents; the mink, river otter, and sea otter among carnivores; and the hippopotamus. Of these species, however, only the sea otter is truly marine.

The early history of the Pacific Coast of North America was greatly influenced by its marine mammal populations. The discovery of the sea otter and the northern fur seal around the middle of the eighteenth century by the expedition under the command of Vitus Bering led to the exploration of western North America by the Russians from Alaska south to California. In their search for the fur of these animals the Russians moved steadily southward until they reached the central California coast, where they built Fort Ross in Sonoma County in 1812. The Russians, with their Aleut assistants, took large numbers of otter and seal pelts from our coastal waters in the early part of the nineteenth century. American fur hunters also slaughtered sea otters and seals, so that the populations of marine fur bearers were vastly reduced prior to the beginning of the twentieth century. Subsequent legislative protection has finally resulted in an increase in the numbers of most species.

Whaling activities were also carried on along the California coast by the start of the nineteenth century, but the first shore whaling station was not established until 1851. This was at Fields Landing near Eureka, Humboldt County, where it operated off and on for over a hundred years. The principal whaling station in central California in the early part of the twentieth century was at Moss Landing along the shore of Monterey Bay. A whaling station operated in San Francisco Bay in recent years, but in 1971 the U.S. Department of Commerce ordered a ban on all commercial whaling by United States vessels.

Most conservationists wish that all whaling could be discontinued, but it is still extensively engaged in by some countries in arctic and antarctic waters. Certain species of whales are protected and one or two are increasing in numbers, but others, especially the larger ones, are rapidly approaching extinction. In the days of the oil lamp, oil from whales, seals, and sea lions was essential to man's well-being. Today, however, to use these animals for nonessentials such as animal food, fertilizer, and the manufacture of plastics hardly seems justified.

The brain of cetaceans is quite large, and these animals have a high level of intelligence. Some of the medium-sized and small cetaceans can be maintained in captivity and taught to perform various feats.

WHERE TO OBSERVE MARINE MAMMALS

From November to February the southward migration of the gray whales may be observed daily from vantage positions along the California coast or from excursion boats that take groups out to sea. Sighting of whales has become a tourist attraction at San Diego. Both the southward migration in late autumn and early winter and the northward movement in late February and March can be seen along many other parts of the coast. Promontories such as Point Loma, Point Sur, Pigeon Point, Point Reyes, or Patricks Point are especially good for viewing the whale migration when the weather is clear.

Sport fishing boats often encounter schools of porpoises, dolphins, and occasionally pilot whales a few miles offshore, and even the larger cetaceans are sometimes seen.

Dead whales and smaller cetaceans often wash into shore. Their presence should always be reported to the nearest museum. Most of the records of our rarest marine mammals have been obtained as a result of observers notifying the nearest proper institution of the presence of a stranded animal. Some institutions which the finder of an unknown dead cetacean might contact are: the Department of Zoology, Humboldt State College, Arcata; the California Academy of Sciences, Golden Gate Park, San Francisco; the Museum of Vertebrate Zoology, University of California, Berkeley; Moss Landing Marine Laboratories; the Santa Barbara Museum of Natural History; the Los Angeles County Museum of Natural History, Exposition Park, Los Angeles; and the San Diego Natural History Museum, Balboa Park, San Diego.

Sea otters may be observed best around the Monterey Peninsula and just to the south at Point Lobos State Park. They also can be seen at a number of localities south along the coast to San Luis Obispo County. They prefer areas where there are large kelp beds and usually stay within several hundred yards of shore.

The California coast provides some of the finest places to observe seals and sea lions outside of the arctic and antarctic regions. Six species are known to occur here. Harbor seals are found locally along the entire coast and may be observed in bays, coves, on rocky reefs, and sand spits. Elephant seals breed on some of the Santa Barbara Channel Islands and on Año Nuevo Island off the southern San Mateo County coast. They are present in varying numbers all year round

[7]

and occasionally haul out on the Farallon Islands. California sea lions breed on the Santa Barbara Channel Islands, and large numbers, principally males, move northward at the end of summer. They may be observed and heard barking nearly anywhere along shore from as far north as British Columbia south to Baja California. Their presence, along with Steller's sea lions, at Seal Rocks is a great attraction in San Francisco. One of the largest Steller's sea lion rookeries outside of Alaska is on Año Nuevo Island. A few Steller's sea lions breed south to San Nicolas Island in the Channel group. Outside of the breeding season individuals may be seen hauled out on offshore rocks and islands along the central and northern California coast. Although the northern fur seal commonly winters offshore, it rarely comes to land and hence is seldom seen. The Guadalupe fur seal is still exceedingly scarce and has been observed by very few persons in southern California.

WHALES, PORPOISES, AND DOLPHINS
ORDER CETACEA

Cetaceans are highly specialized aquatic mammals, believed to have developed from primitive terrestrial ancestors more than seventy million years ago. Morphologically they are recognized by their hairless, streamlined bodies with the forelimbs modified into paddle-like flippers. External vestiges of hind limbs are lacking. The tail is horizontally flattened and has lateral extensions called flukes. A dorsal fin may or may not be present. The surface of the body lacks the usual sebaceous glands that lubricate the hair and skin of land mammals. Likewise, sweat glands and scent glands are absent. Even the nipples of the mammary glands of the female are retracted into slits on either side of the vent when not in use. The ear lacks an external pinna, and the nostrils in all living cetaceans are situated on top of the head, rather posterior in position in all except the sperm whale. The nostril opening is called a blowhole. Externally there is a pair of blowholes in the baleen whales and a single opening in the toothed cetaceans. The upper and lower jaws are very elongate.

Cetaceans have developed many physiological adaptations to life in water. Beneath the skin is a thick layer of fat and connective tissue called blubber, which provides insulation against heat loss to the water. In some of the smaller species blubber may account for more than a third of the body weight.

The respiratory and circulatory systems are specialized to withstand long periods under water. The relative lung capacity of porpoises and dolphins is one and a half times that of terrestrial mammals, but that of the larger, deep-diving whales is only about half that of land mammals. The vascular system in the lung is more involved and the number of red blood corpuscles per cubic millimeter is twice that of terrestrial mammals, thereby facilitating transportation of oxygen and carbon dioxide to and from the tissues.

Furthermore cetaceans appear to be relatively insensitive to carbon dioxide. When a cetacean is submerged its pulse rate generally drops to about half of what it may be when the animal is at the surface. Circulatory shunts automatically reduce blood flow to certain parts of the body during dives, thereby insuring a sufficient supply of oxygen to vital organs such as the brain and heart. Although many of the smaller cetaceans rarely go more than 15 to 20 seconds without coming to the surface to breathe, some of the larger deep-diving species like the sperm whale may stay under for more than an hour and dive to depths of over 3,000 feet.

Locomotion in cetaceans takes place primarily by vertical movement of the posterior part of the body. Strong muscular action accomplishes this, and the broad flukes provide the push which moves the body forward. The flippers function as stabilizers but provide essentially no propelling force.

[9]

Cetaceans surface principally to breathe, and apparently they have no sense of smell. Sight is well developed in many species, although it is reduced in others, especially in those inhabiting turbid water.

In recent years it has been demonstrated that sounds covering a broad range of frequencies are produced by many kinds of cetaceans. In the large baleen whales these are thought to function largely for social communication. In the toothed cetaceans underwater sounds are also employed in orientation and food-finding. The sound pulses for this purpose are produced in nasal sacs and beamed in a specific direction. It has been suggested by some that the concave shape of the skull in the nasal area may serve as a sound reflector, and the so-called "melon" on the forehead focuses the beam. The echoes of such pulses are thought to be transmitted to the internal ears, at least in part, through the lower jaw. The posterior end of the lower jaw terminates next to the ear bones. It is also thought that the small external auditory canal serves to direct sounds to the middle and inner ear. The tympanic bone, which houses the inner ear, is suspended from the skull by ligaments and is housed in a foam-filled cavity. This insulation permits sound to be directed to the inner ear through the auditory canal and ossicles of the middle ear. Since the specific gravity of the body and of water is very similar, sound could enter the ear through any part of the body and disrupt accurate orientation if the auditory organs were not insulated.

The gestation period is long in all cetaceans, varying from 10 to 16 months depending on the species. The female usually has a single young, which grows rapidly on the fat, rich milk.

It is customary to divide the living cetaceans into two major groups, the baleen or whalebone whales and the toothed cetaceans. Some scientists place these groups in separate orders, but they are generally classified as suborders of the order Cetacea, which is the system followed here.

BALEEN OR WHALEBONE WHALES:
SUBORDER MYSTICETI

The baleen whales are mostly large whales that lack any vestige of teeth. Their name is derived from the presence of rows of long, flexible plates that hang down from the roof of the mouth, numbering several hundred, which are known as baleen or whalebone. The margin of each plate is frayed into a hairlike fringe, and the action of these fringed plates serves as a food strainer. The food of baleen whales consists of planktonic organisms, especially small crustaceans (called krill) that abound in polar seas and sometimes small schooling fish. Water is taken into the mouth in the feeding process and the food organisms strained out. Members of the family known as rorquals have accordion-pleated throats that expand greatly to allow large quantities of water to be taken in at one time, thus increasing the efficiency of the straining mechanism. The baleen plates are very long in the bowhead and right whales, in the former measuring as much as 14 feet in length. In the little piked whale, which is the smallest of the rorquals, the baleen is about 20 inches long. It is even shorter in the gray whale.

Baleen whales, unlike the toothed whales, have two external blowholes on the top of the head. These cetaceans range in length from 20 feet for the pigmy right whale (*Caperea marginata*) of the southern hemisphere to about 100 feet for the blue whale (*Balaenoptera musculus*), which is found in all the oceans of the world. Blue whales may attain a weight of nearly 150 tons. In all species of baleen whales the females average larger than the males.

The ten living species of baleen whales are grouped into three families: the right whales (Balaenidae), the gray whale (Eschrichtiidae), and the rorquals (Balaenopteridae). Seven of the ten species have been recorded along the California coast and an eighth, Bryde's

[11]

whale, is known to occur off the coast of Baja California and probably ranges at times as far north as California.

RIGHT WHALES
FAMILY BALAENIDAE

Right whales have a rather stout body with a large head and strongly arched jaws. The throat and anterior underparts lack grooves, and in all except the pigmy right whale of the southern hemisphere a dorsal fin is absent. A distinctive skeletal feature is the fusion of all seven of the cervical vertebrae. Only one member of this family is known to occur off the California coast.

Northern right whale *(Balaena glacialis)*

Total length, up to 60 feet; head very large, constituting about 30 percent of length; dorsal fin absent; mouth strongly arched; body color blackish, sometimes with light patches, particularly on throat; a few warty prominences on lips and snout; baleen blackish and very long, up to 8 or 10 feet in length.

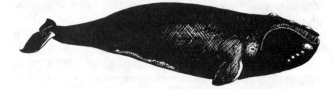

Fig. 1. Northern right whale, *Balaena glacialis*

The Pacific population of the northern right whale summers north to Bering Sea and possibly to the Arctic Ocean but moves southward to winter as far as the coast of Japan in the western Pacific and the Baja California coast in the eastern Pacific. In the early days of whaling in the North Pacific this species was eagerly sought for its high yield of oil. Because it is slow moving and does not sink when killed, the species was brought close to extinction by the whalers. Today right whales are still scarce, although there are a few recent records of sightings off central and southern California.

GRAY WHALE
FAMILY ESCHRICHTIIDAE

The family Eschrichtiidae contains a single species whose present range is limited to the North Pacific Ocean. Subfossil remains indicate that the same species once occurred in the North Atlantic but became extinct about 1500 years ago.

Fig. 2. Gray whale, *Eschrichtius gibbosus*

Gray whale (*Eschrichtius gibbosus*)

Total length, up to 45 or 50 feet; head smaller than in right whales; dorsal fin absent; posterior dorsal ridge on back with a number of small humps; two to four grooves up to 5 feet long on throat; body mottled gray in color; baleen short, less than 20 inches in length, and ivory colored.

Most gray whales feed on amphipods in the Bering and Chukchi seas during the months of June to October. In autumn the southward migration starts. A small population that summers in the Okhotsk Sea moves down the Asiatic coast as far as Korea. The majority migrate south in the eastern Pacific rather close to the North American shoreline. They pass along the coast of California during December and January en route to their calving grounds in the shallow lagoons and protected bays on the west side of Baja California and a few lagoons along the mainland coast of Mexico. The best known calving area is Scammon Lagoon, about 400

[13]

miles south of San Diego. In migration the pregnant females appear first, followed by nonpregnant females and males. During the southward movement they usually stay close to land and so it is easy to see these gray, mottled cetaceans from prominent headlands and fishing or sightseeing boats. After the young are born in January and February they grow rapidly and are ready to travel north with their mothers by March. The newly pregnant females begin their trip earlier, in February, followed by adult males and, later, immatures of both sexes.

Essentially no food is taken during the southward and northward migrations or in the wintering areas. Nonpregnant females are impregnated during the southward migration or close to the calving grounds and bear young about thirteen months later. The young are about 16 feet long at time of birth and are weaned at approximately seven months, when their body length is about 27 feet. Sexual maturity is attained at an average age of eight years.

It is estimated that the eastern Pacific gray whale population numbered somewhere between 25,000 and 30,000 in the early days. Unfortunately intensive slaughter of this slow-moving species during migration and at the calving grounds nearly brought about its extinction. Before the middle of the twentieth century only a small number of gray whales was estimated to exist. Careful protection in recent years has resulted in an increase in the population. Although present estimates vary considerably depending upon the methods employed in censusing, it is probable that there are between 6,000 and 8,000 individuals in the eastern Pacific today.

RORQUALS
FAMILY BALAENOPTERIDAE

The family Balaenopteridae contains the rorquals and the humpback whale. Among them are the giants of the sea, including the blue whale, which is the largest animal ever to exist. They differ from the other baleen whales in having a throat and ventral thoracic region that is grooved or pleated to allow for great expansion when water is taken into the mouth to be strained for krill and other organisms in the feeding process. Members of this family all possess a dorsal fin which distinguishes them from all other baleen whales except the pigmy right whale. The cervical vertebrae, unlike those of right whales, are not fused together.

The rorquals, which include the blue, the finback, the sei, and the minke or piked whale, all have proportionately small heads and trim, streamlined bodies adapted for speed in the water. Because of their speed and the fact that they sink when killed, they escaped the early whalers, but modern whaling methods have greatly reduced their numbers. Some species may soon become extinct unless given total protection. The humpback differs from true rorquals in having a stockier body and very large, knobby flippers. Five species have definitely been recorded in California waters.

Blue whale (*Balaenoptera musculus*)

Total length may exceed 100 feet; ventral grooves extending considerably posterior to level of flippers; dorsal fin relatively small, situated far posterior on back; general body color slate blue above and below, often spotted with lighter patches; baleen black.

Fig. 3. Blue whale, *Balaenoptera musculus*

The blue whale is a cosmopolitan species that is rarely seen along the California coast. In fact, the world population of blue whales is now thought to number less than a thousand individuals. The name sulphur-bottom whale has often been used for this species. This was derived from the yellow color on the body of many of these animals as a result of growths of diatoms acquired in antarctic and arctic waters during the summer feeding periods. Like most large whales, they feed largely in cold polar seas and then move to temperate or subtropical waters to bear their young.

From the commercial viewpoint this is the most valuable of all whales because of its enormous size and high yield of oil. Unfortunately, its value has been responsible for its near extinction.

Fin whale *(Balaenoptera physalus)*

Total length, up to 80 feet; general body shape similar to that of blue whale but somewhat slimmer; dorsal fin larger than that of blue whale; upper parts grayish black, sometimes mottled; ventral surface white; lower jaw asymmetrically colored, with left side pigmented and right side white; baleen blue-gray except for anteriormost plates on right side, which are yellowish white.

Fig. 4.   Fin whale, *Balaenoptera physalus*

The finback, which is the second largest living whale, can readily be distinguished from the blue whale by its white ventral surface and peculiar asymmetrical coloration of the lower jaw and baleen.

Fin whales are the most common of the baleen whales along the California coast, and a small population is known to be present at some seasons of the year in the Gulf of California. The species is cosmopolitan and exhibits a migratory pattern like the blue whale but does not seem to move with as much regularity. This is the most important commercial species in the Antarctic, but the enormous annual catch (26,364 in 1961, for example) is rapidly reducing its numbers. In the North Pacific finback whales range from Bering Sea south to below 20 degrees north latitude.

Sei whale *(Balaenoptera borealis)*

Total length, up to 60 feet, most sexually mature individuals ranging from 40 to 50 feet; body shape in general similar to that of fin whale but ventral grooves not extending as far back, terminating anterior to umbilicus; body color, blue-gray above, becoming white or pinkish ventrally but not on underside of flippers, posterior body, or flukes; baleen black with hairlike fringes whitish.

Fig. 5. Sei whale, *Balaenoptera borealis*

The sei whale is the smallest of the commercially important species of rorquals and has been taken in large numbers in the Antarctic only in recent years as a result of the reduction in the populations of the larger whales. Its distribution in the North Pacific is somewhat similar to that of the fin whale, but it barely gets into the southern part of Bering Sea and does not extend much farther south than 25 degrees north latitude. It is not uncommon along the California coast, where it may be distinguished from the blue and fin whales by smaller size, the white color on the anterior ventral part of the body but not on the posterior parts nor on the underside of the flippers or flukes, and by the whitish fringe on the dark baleen.

Another species known as Bryde's whale *(Balaenoptera edeni)* has been reported off Baja California and in the northwest Pacific. This whale of tropical seas and the southern hemisphere resembles the sei whale but is slimmer and has ventral grooves that extend back to the

[17]

umbilicus. A distinctive feature is the presence of ridges on each side of the head extending from the tip of the snout to the blow holes. Little is known about it.

Minke or little piked whale *(Balaenoptera acutorostrata)*

Total length, up to 30 feet; body shape similar to that of other rorquals but size much smaller; body color blue-gray above, white below; upper side of flipper with white patch or stripe; baleen very short and yellow.

Fig. 6. Minke whale, *Balaenoptera acutorostrata*

This species is common in both the northern and southern hemispheres. This is partly a result of its small size and low oil yield, making it one of the less desirable species for commercial whalers. In the North Pacific this smallest of rorquals moves up into the Bering Sea and the Arctic Ocean to feed in the summer months, and later in the year migrates southward along the Asiatic coast to Japan and along the North American coast as far as the tip of Baja California.

The minke or little piked whale is distinguished by its small size, short, dull yellow baleen, and white patch on the flippers.

Humpback whale *(Megaptera novaeangliae)*

Total length, up to about 50 feet; body thickset in contrast to true rorquals; dorsal fin small and humplike; flippers very large, almost a third as long as body; ventral grooves fewer in number than in true rorquals; conspicuous knobs or protuberances on margins of upper and lower jaws, on flippers, and on back between dorsal fin and flukes; color variable but upper parts generally black and underparts white; baleen black.

[18]

Fig. 7. Humpback whale, *Megaptera novaeangliae*

The humpback whale is easily recognizable by its stocky body, enormous flippers, and numerous knobby protuberances. Its habit of occasionally leaping entirely out of the water and landing with a great splash is also most distinctive.

Humpback whales are cosmopolitan and although their oil yield is relatively low, they have been hunted very heavily because of their size. Their numbers are so low at present that the species is legally given complete protection in the Antarctic.

Humpbacks engage in very regular migrations. In the North Pacific the species summers as far north as the Arctic Ocean but moves far southward in the breeding season. Along the Asiatic coast their range extends south to the Philippine Basin, and along the Pacific Coast of North America they are recorded to the tip of Baja California and in the Gulf of California. The species is frequently seen during migration off the California coast.

TOOTHED CETACEANS:
SUBORDER ODONTOCETI

The toothed cetaceans or odontocetes include the sperm whales, the beaked whales, the beluga and narwhal, the killer whale, and the porpoises and dolphins. All have teeth in one or both jaws, the number varying from 2 to over 200. Although the great majority of toothed cetaceans are much smaller than the baleen whales, the food they consume is much larger and consists of fish and cephalopods.

[19]

The external nasal passages of odontocetes are joined to form a single blowhole, unlike the paired blowholes of the baleen whales. The single external orifice is usually crescentic or horizontal, but in the Ganges River dolphin it is elongate. In some species the rostral and frontal region of the head are greatly enlarged. The extreme may be seen in the sperm whale. In others the mouth is extended forward as a sort of long, narrow beak. This condition is seen in some of the dolphins and beaked whales. The skulls of toothed whales are asymmetrical, unlike those of baleen whales.

The toothed cetaceans show great variation in size, ranging from the sperm whale, which may attain a length of 60 feet, to slightly more than 4 feet in the smallest dolphins and porpoises.

Currently there are about seventy-four living kinds of toothed cetaceans, grouped into at least seven different families, as follows: the beaked whales (Ziphiidae), the narwhal and beluga (Monodontidae), the sperm whales (Physeteridae), the long-snouted river dolphins (Platanistidae), the rough-toothed, river, and coastal dolphins (Stenidae), the porpoises (Phocoenidae), and the ocean dolphins (Delphinidae). About eighteen kinds of odontocetes have been recorded from the California coast.

BEAKED WHALES
FAMILY ZIPHIIDAE

Beaked whales are small to medium in size (15 to 42 feet in length) with elongate, beaklike mouths. Except for one genus (*Tasmacetus*) known from a few specimens from New Zealand, beaked whales have the teeth reduced to one or two visible pairs in the lower jaw, although additional small, vestigial teeth may be embedded in the gums. In some species the teeth are very large, while in others they do not break through the gums. The latter situation most often occurs in females, in which the teeth are always smaller. The throat of ziphiid whales is marked by two longitudinal grooves that converge anteriorly. A small dorsal fin is located relatively far back on the body, and the tail flukes lack a median notch. Three kinds of beaked whales have been recorded along the California coast.

Baird's beaked whale *(Berardius bairdii)*

Total length, up to 42 feet; body blackish or grayish brown above and grayish white, sometimes mottled, on underside; frontal part of head rather prominent and bulging; two pairs of prominent teeth, laterally compressed, at tip of lower jaw in males; two pairs of teeth in females, often hidden beneath gums.

Fig. 8. Baird's beaked whale, *Berardius bairdii*

Baird's beaked whale is exceeded in size among toothed cetaceans only by the sperm whale. It is occasionally taken by whalers and referred to as the bottle-nosed whale, although this name properly refers to members of another genus of beaked whale, *Hyperoodon*, which has not been recorded along the Pacific Coast of North America. Baird's beaked whale is not sought after because of its relatively small size. It is known from the central California coast northward to southern Alaska and the southern part of Bering Sea. The species also ranges southward along the Asiatic coast to southern Japan. Its food appears to consist largely of squid. There is one other species belonging to this genus, the large beaked whale *(Berardius arnouxi)* that occurs in oceans of the southern hemisphere.

[21]

Stejneger's beaked whale *(Mesoplodon stejnegeri)*

Total length, up to about 17 feet; body rather stout, blackish above and below except for beak, which is white; surface usually marked by numerous white scars in form of lines and oval patches; two prominent teeth in lower jaw of male, extending up on either side of rostrum; each tooth up to 5 inches in height with prominent tip, about 3 inches in length and half an inch in breadth.

Fig. 9. Stejneger's beaked whale, *Mesoplodon stejnegeri,* male

This is one of the rarest as well as most distinctive cetaceans recorded from California. It is known from several specimens washed ashore from San Diego northward. No one has positively seen this species alive. The dark body, white beak, and two enormous teeth that extend upward outside the mouth when the jaws are closed, are distinctive characters for identification. The author is of the opinion that it is closely related to *Mesoplodon bowdoini* of the southern hemisphere—perhaps a northern subspecies. *M. carlhubbsi* was named a few years ago from a stranded beaked whale in southern California, but it is questionably distinguishable from *M. stejnegeri.*

The only information relative to the food of this species is based on the presence of squid beaks found in the stomach of a stranded individual.

Cuvier's beaked whale *(Ziphius cavirostris)*

Total length, up to about 28 feet; general body color, black or blackish, usually with numerous white scars;

head and anterior back whitish, at least in adult male; beak prominent; male with one pair of large, protruding teeth, round or oval in cross section, at tip of lower jaw; teeth in female small, embedded in gum.

Fig. 10.   Cuvier's beaked whale, *Ziphius cavirostris,* male

Cuvier's beaked whale has been recorded from the Gulf of California northward along the Pacific Coast to the Bering Sea and south along the coast of Asia to southern Japan. It also occurs in the Atlantic Ocean and in seas of the southern hemisphere. It is a relatively large species although smaller than Baird's beaked whale, from which it may readily be distinguished by the teeth, which are two in number instead of four, and essentially round in cross section rather than laterally compressed. It is taken commercially in Japan.

SPERM WHALES
FAMILY PHYSETERIDAE

Two kinds of toothed whales are included in the family Physeteridae. One of them is *Physeter catodon,* the sperm whale. The other includes the two closely related species of pigmy sperm whales belonging to the genus *Kogia.* Functional teeth are present only in the lower jaw in sperm whales. Only the left nasal passage serves for respiration, and the external blowhole is displaced to the left side of the head. The front or rostral portion of the skull is very broad and flat.

Sperm whale *(Physeter catodon)*

Total length, up to 60 feet for males and 30 to 40 feet for females; head very large and blunt-ended, constitut-

[23]

ing about a third of body length; blowhole at tip of snout; lower jaw very narrow in proportion to head size; dorsal fin absent although represented by hump; general body color bluish gray to purplish brown above, becoming paler on underparts.

The sperm whale is the giant of the toothed cetaceans, but very large size is attained only by the males. This marked difference in size of males and females is unusual in cetaceans. The enormous head of the sperm whale contains a large reservoir of oil-like substance known as spermaceti. The function of the spermaceti organ, or "case" as it is called by whalers, is not known, although it is suspected to play a part in the very deep dives in which these animals engage. It may possibly function for sound transmission like the bulging forehead or "melon" of some other cetaceans.

The terminal blowhole is unique among cetaceans. In other species the blowhole or holes are situated more posteriorly on the top of the head. Because of the anterior position of the blowhole, the spout in this species is directed forward rather than vertically.

Fig. 11.   Sperm whale, *Physeter catodon*

Sperm whales are widely distributed over the oceans of the world, although there is a seasonal difference in the distribution of males and females, the former going almost to the polar seas in summer while the females stay in tropical, subtropical, or temperate waters and do not venture beyond 40 degrees north or south latitude.

Recent studies have shown that the period of pregnancy for this species averages 14.6 months and lactation lasts for about two years. By the time the calf is weaned it is about 25 feet long. Following lactation the female has a rest period of nine months before the beginning of the next pregnancy. The female reproductive cycle, therefore, is about four years.

The food of sperm whales consists principally of large species of squid. Scars from the suckers of these giant cephalopods are frequently seen on the bodies of the whales.

The sperm whale has long been sought after by whalers because of its high oil yield and especially because of the spermaceti in the head. Another product obtained from it is ambergris, which is a peculiar substance derived from the intestinal tract and was formerly in high demand as a perfume fixative. Ambergris when fresh is waxy and foul smelling; when dry it is brittle and crumbles easily. When penetrated by a hot needle it adheres to the latter as a sticky, blackish liquid, thus readily distinguished from paraffin, which often floats up on beaches and is mistaken for the cetacean product. Ambergris today is largely replaced by synthetic fixatives in the perfume industry.

Sperm whales were taken in large numbers along the California coast in years past. Today, however, their population is much reduced.

Pigmy sperm whale *(Kogia breviceps)*

Total length, up to about 13 feet; head blunt; lower jaw small, triangular, not reaching to tip of snout, thereby producing sharklike appearance; small, functional teeth in lower jaw; upper jaw with very small, nonfunctional teeth deeply embedded in gum tissue; small dorsal fin in middle of back; blowhole displaced slightly to left side of head but not as far forward as in sperm whale; color blackish above, becoming pale beneath.

Fig. 12. Pigmy sperm whale, *Kogia breviceps*, subadult

It appears possible that there may be two species of
pigmy sperm whales, *Kogia breviceps* and *K. simus*, but
very little is known about these rare cetaceans. Pigmy
sperm whales have been found in the Pacific, Atlantic,
and Indian oceans, but only in temperate and subtropical waters. In the North Pacific specimens have been
recorded along the American coast from Washington,
California, and Baja California. Along the Asiatic coast
pigmy sperm whales are known from Japan southward.

A stranded pigmy sperm whale that washed up on
Point Reyes, Marin County, in December 1968, was
found to have eaten squid, as indicated by numerous
beaks of these cephalopods in its stomach.

ROUGH-TOOTHED, RIVER, AND
COASTAL DOLPHINS
FAMILY STENIDAE

The family Stenidae was proposed in 1960 to include
the rough-toothed dolphin and species of the genera
Sousa and *Sotalia*, which live in coastal waters and
estuaries or even the lower parts of major rivers of
South America, Asia, and Africa. They differ from other
kinds of dolphins in the structure of the air sinus system.

Rough-toothed dolphin *(Steno bredanensis)*

Total length, up to 8 feet; no noticeable break between elongate beak and forehead; dorsal fin present;
upper surface bluish gray to purplish black with few
scattered whitish marks; underparts white or pinkish

[26]

with some scattered dark patches; 20 to 24 pairs of fairly large teeth with rough crown surface resulting from presence of fine vertical ridges; mandibular symphysis more than 30 percent of length of mandibles; first two cervical vertebrae fused together.

Fig. 13. Rough-toothed dolphin, *Steno bredanensis*

Very little is known of the distribution of this rather rare dolphin other than that it occurs in tropical to temperate seas. It is not common in the North Pacific. The writer recorded the only specimen from the west coast of North America in 1951. This was based on a skull found washed up on Stinson Beach, Marin County, California, by Edward P. Davies. Individuals are occasionally taken off the coast of Japan.

The rough surface of the teeth readily distinguishes this species from all other kinds of small cetaceans.

PORPOISES
FAMILY PHOCOENIDAE

Members of the porpoise family do not have the elongated snout that is characteristic of so many of the ocean dolphins. Furthermore they are small in size and have spatulate or spadelike teeth instead of pointed, conical teeth. Three to seven of their cervical vertebrae may be fused together. Porpoises are strictly coastal in distribution and frequently enter bays and estuaries. There are only three genera of porpoises, two of which are represented by one species each along the California coast.

[27]

Harbor porpoise *(Phocoena phocoena)*

Total length, up to 6 feet; body stout, snout blunt and rounded; dorsal fin small and triangular; 22 to 27 pairs of spade-shaped teeth in each jaw; color tending to be black or blackish above, gray to white on underparts; rather weakly defined dark stripe extending from corner of mouth to front base of flipper.

Fig. 14.   Harbor porpoise, *Phocoena phocoena*

This is the smallest cetacean to be found in California waters. Its size, blunt nose, dark dorsal coloration, and spade-shaped teeth distinguish it from any other small porpoises or dolphins. Harbor porpoises are occasionally seen in San Francisco Bay and are commonly observed by fishermen off the coast. In the Pacific this species ranges from Alaskan waters south to coastal southern California and along the Asiatic coast south to Japan. Another species, *Phocoena sinus,* occurs in the Gulf of California, Mexico, but little is known about its external appearance. Its skull is readily distinguishable from that of the harbor porpoise by the broader base to the rostrum. Two other species are found in the southern hemisphere.

Dall's porpoise *(Phocoenoides dalli)*

Total length, 6 to 7 feet; body stout, snout blunt; dorsal fin triangular but slightly hooked at apex; prominent hump on lower back between dorsal fin and flukes; teeth spade-shaped; color, grayish black with conspicuous white lateral patch extending up from belly to either side of body; dorsal fin and tail flukes usually rimmed with white.

Fig. 15.   Dall's porpoise, *Phocoenoides dalli*

The small size and conspicuous black and white color pattern make Dall's porpoise one of the easiest cetaceans to identify. It is larger than the harbor porpoise, usually weighing over 200 pounds as contrasted with about 160 pounds for the smaller species. Furthermore, it does not normally enter bays and estuaries but stays on the outer coast within 20 miles of shore. The species ranges northward from northern Baja California to Alaska and south along the coast of Asia to Japan.

Dall's porpoises travel in small groups, usually consisting of ten to fifteen individuals. They are capable of swimming very rapidly. Attempts have been made to keep these strikingly colored porpoises in captivity, but so far without success.

OCEAN DOLPHINS
FAMILY DELPHINIDAE

The Delphinidae is the largest cetacean family and probably the most difficult one to define clearly. Its members range in size from about 6 feet to 30 feet in length. Some species have a prominent beak, others have a porpoise-like head, and several possess a prominent bulging forehead known as a "melon." Most ocean dolphins have a large number of conical teeth in both jaws. In the grampus or Risso's dolphin, however, teeth are absent from the upper jaw and reduced to two to seven pairs near the tip of the lower jaw. In a number

[29]

of species the males are considerably larger than the females.

North Pacific pilot whale *(Globicephala scammoni)*

Total length, males up to 22 feet, females up to about 16 feet; forehead with prominent "melon" or bulge; dorsal fin large and triangular; flippers relatively long and slender; eight to ten pairs of teeth in each jaw; color, usually black or blackish with lighter area sometimes evident just behind dorsal fin.

Fig. 16.   North Pacific pilot whale, *Globicephala scammoni*, male

Pilot whales are sometimes referred to as blackfish. They are readily recognized by their medium-large size, bulging forehead, long, slender flippers, and black coloration. The name "pilot whale" is probably derived from the habit these cetaceans have of following a leader. They travel in pods of as many as 200 individuals. Occasionally, for reasons not clearly understood, the leaders become stranded on a beach and the rest of the group follow to a similar fate. Such strandings are usually on gently sloping shores with a long patch of shallow water adjacent. It has been suggested that echo-navigation is difficult in such places. Other suggested causes are pathological conditions, hunger, and the desire for warmer waters which are to be found in shallow areas.

Pilot whales are relatively slow swimmers. When a large group is moving the individuals are often arranged in twos and threes. They show little fear of man and permit close approach by boat. In captivity they can readily be trained to perform.

There are believed to be at least two and possibly three species of pilot whales in the world. The North Pacific species, *Globicephala scammoni*, ranges from waters off the coast of northern Baja California north to Alaska and west, generally south of the Aleutian chain, to Asia and then south to northern Japanese waters.

Killer whale *(Orcinus orca)*

Total length, males up to 30 feet, females up to 23 feet; body streamlined with head lacking distinct beak; dorsal fin very large, triangular in male and reaching length of 5 or 6 feet, smaller in female and curved posteriorly; pectoral fins large, rounded; each jaw with 10 to 14 pairs of massive teeth, oval in cross section; upper parts black with white patch extending posteriorly from above eye, white saddle or patches posterior to dorsal fin; ventral parts white with extension coming up on flanks.

Fig. 17. Killer whale, *Orcinus orca*, male

Killer whales are sometimes observed singly, but they usually travel in groups, often dominated by a large male. These are composed of a small number of individuals, but aggregations numbering up to 200 whales have been observed in antarctic waters.

This species has long been regarded as the killer of

[31]

the sea. However, there are no authenticated records of their ever killing human beings. These animals tame rather rapidly in captivity and show a high degree of intelligence, like other cetaceans. Under natural conditions they rove the sea in search of seals, sea lions, walruses, other cetaceans, fish, squid, and marine birds. Their predatory habits and large size account for their rather frightening name.

The only other species with which the killer whale might be confused is the Dall porpoise, which is a much smaller species that lacks the white behind the eye and has only a small, curved dorsal fin.

The killer whale is cosmopolitan in distribution but most abundant in colder waters.

False killer whale *(Pseudorca crassidens)*

Total length, about 18 feet maximum; body proportionally long and streamlined; snout more rounded than in killer whale; head lacking "melon" seen in pilot whale and somewhat depressed in region of blowhole; dorsal fin small, curved posteriorly; flipper relatively small, pointed; about eleven pairs of powerful teeth, round in cross section, in each jaw; body color, black with small, light scars occasionally present.

Fig. 18. False killer whale, *Pseudorca crassidens*

The false killer whale is another nearly cosmopolitan species, but it seems to avoid the polar seas and is more abundant away from continental shorelines. There are a few records for California as well as the Gulf of California. Occasionally groups of false killer whales become stranded. This happened a few years ago on

[32]

Killer whale at Sea World, San Diego

Common dolphins

Fighting Steller's sea lion bulls.

Gray whale "blowing."

Aerial view of gray whale and calf.

Stranded gray whale. (George E. Lindsay)

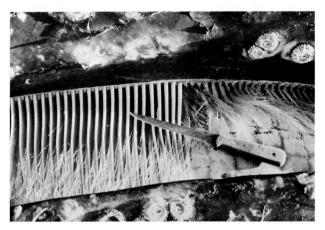

Lateral view of the mouth of a gray whale showing baleen
in upper jaw and barnacles on skin. (Laurence C. Binford)

A finback whale surfacing. (Thomas Tilton)

Head of beached Stejneger's beaked whale.

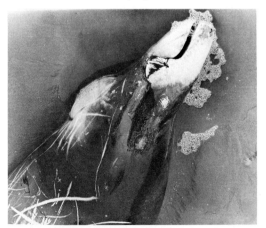

Harbor seals hauled out at low tide.
(Edward S. Ross)

Harbor seals on a ledge below some
Steller's sea lions.

A bull elephant seal.

A young elephant seal threatening.

A bull northern fur seal.

A northern fur seal harem with a
bull, cows, and pups.

Underwater view of a false killer whale (above) and two pilot whales (below). (Courtesy of Marineland of the Pacific, Los Angeles)

Pacific white-sided dolphins in Steinhart Aquarium, San Francisco.

Common dolphins in the Gulf of California. (George E. Lindsay)

Bottlenosed dolphin in Steinhart Aquarium,
San Francisco.

Sea otter feeding. (Karl W. Kenyon)

Guadalupe fur seal on Guadalupe Island.
(George E. Lindsay)

Steller's sea lion cows and pups.

Adult male California sea lions.

A mixed group of California and Steller's sea lions.

the south shore of San José Island in the Gulf of California. Skeletal remains of five individuals stranded in a group were found there and are now in the American Museum of Natural History in New York and the California Academy of Sciences in San Francisco.

False killer whales sometimes travel in groups estimated to contain hundreds or even thousands of individuals. Their food consists principally of fairly large fish such as mahimahi, tuna, and bonita. They adapt rapidly to captivity, learn quickly and are very compatible with other delphinids.

Northern right whale dolphin (*Lissodelphis borealis*)

Total length, up to about 8 feet; body dolphin-like with distinct beak; lower jaw protruding beyond upper jaw; dorsal fin lacking; numerous small, conical teeth in both jaws; upper part of body black; ventral surface, including undersides of flippers and flukes, glossy white.

Fig. 19.   Northern right whale dolphin, *Lissodelphis borealis*

This species is in no way related to the right whales, but like them it lacks a dorsal fin. This feature readily distinguishes the right whale dolphin from all other small toothed cetaceans along the Pacific Coast of North America.

Although there are very few records of strandings for right whale dolphins along the coast of California, fairly large groups are occasionally seen offshore. The northern species is known to range from the Gulf of Alaska south to southern California; in the eastern Pacific they occur off the coast of Japan. Another species, *Lissodelphis peroni*, is known from the southern hemisphere. It differs from *L. borealis* in having the white of the ventral parts extending higher up on the body so as to include the flippers and the beak.

Common dolphin *(Delphinus delphis)*

Total length, up to 7 or 8 feet; body streamlined, with beak set off markedly from rest of head by deep groove; dorsal fin well developed, convex anteriorly and concave behind; each jaw with 46 to 65 pairs of small, conical, sharply pointed teeth; dorsal surface blackish to purplish brown, color extending down below level of anterior base of dorsal fin as wedge to produce saddle-like pattern; ventral surface white; dark line extending from beak to flipper, another dark area surrounding eye; sides of body between dark back and white ventral surface, yellowish gray.

Fig. 20.   Common dolphin, *Delphinus delphis*

The common or saddle-backed dolphin is a cosmopolitan species of temperate and subtropical waters, but it seldom ranges far from continental shore lines. Several distinct populations are recognized. These differ from one another in color pattern and some other characters but are generally regarded as subspecies of *Delphinus delphis*. In the eastern Pacific the common dolphin ranges north to British Columbia. The common dolphin that occurs in the Gulf of California and along the west coast of Baja California is regarded by some cetologists as a separate species, *Delphinus bairdii*. Others consider it a subspecies of *D. delphis*. Until

[34]

about the turn of the century this southern form ranged northward to central California.

Common dolphins have long been known to man and are frequently represented in ancient Grecian art. A famous frieze in the Palace of Knossos on the Island of Crete in the eastern Mediterranean, made about 2000 B.C., depicts these beautiful animals.

These graceful little cetaceans usually travel in very large groups. It is not uncommon along the Pacific Coast of North America or in the Gulf of California to observe aggregations numbering more than 1,000, and in the Black Sea single groups of 100,000 have been observed. They are always conspicuous because of their habit of leaping out of the water. By plane one can sometimes spot a large group many miles away because the sea is churned up as a result of "porpoising" by the dolphins.

Another interesting habit of the common dolphin is swimming by the side of boats, sometimes almost directly under the prow. This seems to be a form of play behavior. Strangely the species does not do well in captivity.

The term dolphin, as applied to small beaked cetaceans, is sometimes confused with the mahimahi or dolphin-fish of the genus *Coryphaena* found in tropical waters.

Risso's dolphin *(Grampus griseus)*

Total length, reported to reach maximum of 11 to 13 feet; head lacking beak, rather bulbous, with "melon" present; flippers of moderate size, somewhat pointed; two to seven pairs of teeth in anterior part of lower jaw; teeth usually absent from upper jaw; color variable, dorsal surface of body and flukes generally dark with sides, underparts pale gray or white; entire body usually streaked with conspicuous white scars, often producing effect of whitish cetacean.

[35]

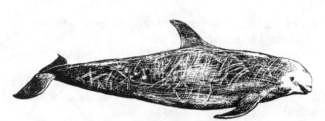

Fig. 21. Risso's dolphin, *Grampus griseus*

Risso's dolphin somewhat resembles the pilot whale in body and head shape but has a higher, more pointed dorsal fin, smaller flippers, a much lighter and noticeably scarred body, and functional teeth in the lower jaw only. It is widely distributed over the world, occurring in temperate waters of both the Atlantic and the Pacific, north and south of the equator, and in the Mediterranean. In the eastern North Pacific Risso's dolphin has been reported from southern British Columbia south to California. It is not a common species, however, and strandings or sightings are rare. This may result from the somewhat solitary habits of this species. Occasionally small groups of up to half a dozen individuals are noted.

Pacific white-sided dolphin *(Lagenorhynchus obliquidens)*

Total length, about 7 feet; head and body streamlined; beak hardly evident; dorsal fin and flippers of moderate size, somewhat pointed; about twenty pairs of sharp, conical teeth in each jaw; bluish gray to black on upper parts, white ventrally with sides grayish white and light streak on either side of posterior part of back; posterior part of dorsal fin light in color.

This is a common species in the North Pacific. Along the west coast of North America white-sided dolphins range from southeastern Alaska to Panama, and in the western Pacific from the Commander Islands south to the Philippines. They are also fairly common in the Central Pacific around Hawaii.

Fig. 22. Pacific white-sided dolphin, *Lagenorhynchus obliqui-
dens*

Pacific white-sided dolphins travel in large schools
and engage in seasonal migrations that seem to be primarily associated with the movements of fishes upon
which they feed. They will follow boats, and they tame
readily in captivity. Observing them in the latter situation one is always amazed at their great speed and body
control under relatively confined conditions. They frequently swim in pairs, exhibiting remarkable synchron-
ization of movement and respiratory behavior, both
usually blowing at the same time.

Eastern Pacific spotted dolphin *(Stenella graffmani)*

Total length, up to about 7 feet; general body shape
similar to that of common dolphin; beak long, conspicuous; dorsal fin and flipper of moderate size, tapering
rather than rounded; numerous small conical teeth in
each jaw; general pattern of body color consisting of a
dark gray saddle extending forward to the head with
lighter underparts. As the animal grows older, spots appear as follows: white on the dark upperparts and gray
on the whitish underparts. Eventually most of the ventral gray spots merge into a solid color with a few white
spots remaining. The result is a dolphin, dark above and
gray below, with white spots over most of the body but
concentrated mainly above the eye and in an area below
the posterior portion of the saddle.

This species is reportedly common in parts of the

[37]

Fig. 23.   Eastern Pacific spotted dolphin, *Stenella graffmani,* male adult

tropical and subtropical eastern Pacific Ocean from the west coast of northern South America to Baja California, Mexico. It is said to be well known to tuna fishermen in those waters, who call it the "spotter porpoise," but little of a scientific nature has been published regarding its habits. Studies are being made on this species by scientists of the U.S. Bureau of Commercial Fisheries at La Jolla. The species has been recorded from southern California.

Eastern Pacific spotted dolphins travel in large schools, some numbering more than 1,000 animals. Their food consists of fish and squid. The long beak combined with numerous light spots on the generally gray-colored body are good field characters for identification.

Blue and white dolphin *(Stenella caeruleoalba)*

Total length, up to 10 feet; similar in body shape to Pacific spotted dolphin, with conspicuous beak and medium sized tapering flippers and dorsal fin; up to fifty pairs of conical teeth, some curved inward, in each jaw; upper parts and tip of beak blackish or dark brown; ventral parts of body white with blackish lines extending from eye to base of flipper and from eye to region of vent.

The classification of blue and white dolphins (often called the "streaker porpoise" by fishermen) in the North Pacific needs further study. These dolphins range northward from the waters off southern California to British Columbia, and a very similar dolphin occurs along the Asiatic coast. Whether there is continuity of range across the North Pacific is not known. For this reason the name *Stenella caeruleoalba* is used here for the eastern Pacific form rather than combined, as done by some authors, with *Stenella styx* (also known as *S. euphrosyne*) of the western Pacific. There are few records for this species for the California coast and little is known regarding its habits.

Fig. 24.   Blue and white dolphin, *Stenella caeruleoalba*

Another species, the long-snouted dolphin (*Stenella longirostris*) or spinner, is commonly encountered by tuna fishermen off the coast of Mexico and southward. It is often found with the eastern Pacific spotted dolphin. Long-snouted dolphins are dark gray to blackish above and somewhat lighter below. When seen close up they have a dark band bordered anteriorly by a lighter gray that extends from the eye to the base of the flipper. The snout is longer in this species than in either of the other two members of the genus *Stenella* described previously. The spinner derives its name from the fact that during its leaps out of water it may rotate sideways, thereby accomplishing a barrel roll.

Pacific bottlenosed dolphin *(Tursiops gillii)*

Total length, up to 12 feet; body relatively large; beak conspicuous but not greatly elongated; about 18 to 25 pairs of stout conical teeth in each jaw; general body color gray, with ventral parts lighter. *T. gillii* differs from *T. truncatus* of the Atlantic Ocean by its slimmer body, darker coloration and stouter teeth. Apart from

[39]

this the two species are similar in markings.

Bottlenosed dolphins are very adaptable to life in captivity and can easily be trained to perform. They are highly intelligent and have been the subjects of numerous studies by biologists. "Flipper," known to millions of Americans, is a bottlenosed dolphin.

Bottlenosed dolphins are widely distributed in temperate, subtropical, and tropical seas. In the eastern Pacific they are known from California south to the equa-

Fig. 25. Pacific bottlenosed dolphin, *Tursiops gillii*

tor. They are also found in the central Pacific around Hawaii, and along the Asiatic coast. Several species of bottlenosed dolphins have been named, and there are decided differences in size and color between different populations.

Bottlenosed dolphins are usually seen in small groups along the coast of California and in the Gulf of California. They are sometimes associated with other species such as the common dolphin and like the latter may swim alongside or ahead of moving vessels. Under such circumstances they frequently leap high out of the water. The large size, stout beak, and rather uniform light gray color are useful features for identification.

CARNIVORES: ORDER CARNIVORA
FAMILY MUSTELIDAE

Sea otter *(Enhydra lutris)*

Total length, up to nearly 5 feet; tail about one-fourth the body length, thick and somewhat flattened; hind

[40]

feet webbed; front feet relatively small and round; head rather round; external ears very small; fur extremely fine and dense; dark brown to nearly black with frosted appearance increasing with age, especially on head of males.

The order to which the sea otter belongs is composed largely of terrestrial mammals that subsist principally on flesh. A few, like the mink (*Mustela vison*) and the various species of river otters, have become semi-aquatic. The polar bear (*Ursus maritimus*) is a regular inhabitant of the sea but spends considerable time on land and on the arctic ice. Only the sea otter is truly marine.

The history of the sea otter has been written many times, because it is intimately connected with the exploration of western North America. The species was first discovered in 1741 by Vitus Bering and his crew. They spent the winter on an island in the North Pacific when one of their ships was forced to land on Bering Island while returning from the coast of America. The men survived because the sea otter and other marine mammals provided them with food and clothing to protect them from the rigorous subarctic climate. When Bering and his crew returned to the China coast the following year the fame of the sea otter began to spread and fabulous sums were offered for its pelt.

Search for sea otter skins for the European and Asian fur trade rapidly led to the exploration of the Aleutian Islands by the Russians. Later they gradually moved down the Pacific Coast to California, where they established Fort Ross in 1812.

The sea otters originally ranged over an area nearly 6,000 miles long from islands off the northern coast of Japan, the Kurile Islands, along the Aleutian chain to the Alaskan Peninsula, and then all the way down to central Baja California, Mexico. Sea otters were reported especially abundant around the Farallon Islands, in San Francisco Bay, and around the Santa Barbara Channel Islands off the southern California coast. Many

[41]

thousands were taken in these areas during the first half of the nineteenth century. However, no fur-bearing mammal could withstand such a heavy harvest. This was especially true of a species whose distribution was limited to the immediate vicinity, generally less than a quarter of a mile, of the coastline of the mainland or adjacent islands. The sea otter population first declined in Alaska, where hundreds of thousands of animals were killed. It is said that the almost complete elimination of sea otters there influenced the Russians to sell this land to the United States in 1867 for $7,200,000, because it then appeared worthless.

Before the beginning of the twentieth century the sea otter was close to extinction and was completely eliminated over most of its formerly extensive range. In 1911 a treaty was signed by the United States, Russia, Japan, and Canada affording sea otters complete protection from commercial exploitation, and in 1913 the Aleutian Islands National Wildlife Refuge was established to give additional safety to the few hundred of the animals remaining in Alaskan waters. Sea otters by this time were gone from southeastern Alaska, British Columbia, and the coasts of Washington and Oregon. A small herd apparently survived along the rather inaccessible coast of Monterey County in central California and was "discovered" in 1938 when the new coast highway connecting Monterey with San Simeon was opened. Through careful protection this herd has increased to over a thousand animals and has expanded its range of the 1930s south to San Luis Obispo County and north to Monterey Bay. Today occasional individuals are seen as far north as Humboldt County, and one was seen in the south near San Diego.

The habits of the sea otter are unique in many respects. It is a member of a family of land carnivores, the Mustelidae, to which weasels, minks, martens, wolverines, badgers, skunks, and their allies belong, yet it literally spends its life in the sea. Sea otters are seldom seen even on offshore rocks along the California coast.

[42]

Apparently the young are even born in the sea.

Adults usually swim or float on their backs. They frequent kelp beds close to shore and dive periodically for food, which consists of crabs, sea urchins, and various other types of shellfish, including abalones. Some commercial fishermen blame the thousand or so sea otters for a reduction in the numbers of abalones, rather than over-exploitation of these mollusks by man. Records show that abalones were abundant along the California coast in the early days when sea otters were present in vastly greater numbers than today.

Sea otters in a sense make use of tools, as do only a very few other kinds of animals. To assist in breaking the hard exoskeleton of certain shellfish, they bring up rocks from the ocean floor and use them to crack the shells by pounding the shellfish on the rock held on their chests while floating on their backs.

These animals spend much of their time cleaning and grooming their thick, dense fur. They also have the habit of winding a strand of kelp about their bodies before they sleep. This prevents them from drifting away from the relative security of the inshore waters. A group of sleeping sea otters that have anchored themselves in this manner will all have their bodies oriented in the same direction because of currents or wind.

The principal enemies of sea otters, apart from man, are sharks and killer whales. Autopsies on several dead individuals found on the shore of Monterey Bay have revealed tooth marks and, in one instance, even a tooth itself of a man-eater shark.

The best places to observe these fascinating animals are at Point Lobos State Park or along the Seventeen Mile Drive on the Monterey Peninsula. Sometimes they may be seen from the wharf at Monterey or along the shore near Pacific Grove.

SEALS AND SEA LIONS
ORDER PINNIPEDIA

Pinnipeds, like cetaceans, are remarkably adapted to

life in the sea. Their bodies are streamlined, the somewhat fusiform shape offering minimum resistance to passage through water. External ears are greatly reduced, with the pinna absent in the hair seals. The eyes are large and well adapted to see under water. The limbs are modified into flippers by shortening of the bones of the front and hind legs, which are partly within the body, and elongation of the fingers and toes, which are joined together by connective tissue and skin to form broad propelling surfaces. The tail is extremely short.

Pinniped skin is quite thick and well haired except in the walrus, whose hair is sparse. Beneath the skin, as in cetaceans, is a layer of fat, which provides insulation for the body. Since the majority of seals and sea lions, as well as the walrus, inhabit the colder oceans of the world, the problem of regulating body temperature is an important one. Their internal temperature is essentially constant and about that of the human species. The skin and flippers are provided with well-developed capillary networks. When the body becomes overheated, blood passing rapidly through these tiny channels near the surface is cooled. When the body temperature drops, the flow of blood to the peripheral areas is reduced and body heat conserved. The temperature of the skin in arctic species may at times be close to that of the water while that of the rest of the animal inside the layer of blubber is at the typical mammalian level. On land the large flippers of the northern fur seal are regularly waved in a fanlike manner to help keep the body temperature down.

Pinnipeds can stay under water for relatively long periods of time, and some species may make extremely deep dives. The Weddell seal of the Antarctic can descend to a depth of 1,400 feet beneath the surface. This entails going without breathing for many minutes while the body is exerting itself considerably. Seals and sea lions do not accomplish this by having larger lungs than land mammals or a greater oxygen-carrying capacity.

[44]

Instead, they have developed valves in various parts of the circulatory system which shut down the supply of blood to many parts of the body and insure sufficient oxygen for the brain and heart. Likewise, during a dive, the heart beat is reduced to about one-tenth of that normal on the surface. These diving mammals are much more tolerant of high concentrations of carbon dioxide in the body than are land mammals.

Recent studies have shown that many kinds of pinnipeds are capable of producing underwater sounds. These may function for communication to some extent, but it is possible that they may serve for echo-ranging. At night or at depths where visibility is limited these underwater sounds could aid in orientation and in the location of food in a method somewhat similar to that used by cetaceans and bats.

There are thirty-one living species of pinnipeds, most of which are restricted to the polar and subpolar areas. Six of these are found along the California coast, of which four are representatives of the family Otariidae, the sea lions and fur seals, sometimes called the eared seals because they have a small external ear. The other two species belong to the Phocidae, the hair seals or earless seals which lack an external pinna to the ear. The only other pinniped family is the Odobenidae, to which the walrus belongs. This is restricted to arctic and subarctic waters.

EARED SEALS
FAMILY OTARIIDAE

The family Otariidae contains the sea lions and fur seals. All of its members have hind flippers that can be brought under the hind part of the body and used for locomotion on land. The nails of the three middle digits of the hind flippers are well developed, but those of the outer two are rudimentary. The external ears, although not large, are easily seen. The front flippers are proportionately large and naked and are the primary means of propulsion.

[45]

Eared seals are found in the subpolar regions of both hemispheres as well as in temperate and even subtropical waters. They tend to be coastal in distribution, but the northern fur seal is pelagic during part of the year. All species have a well-developed social system during the breeding period when they come to land. Only mature, dominant bulls acquire harems of females. There is marked sexual dimorphism in size in all members of the family, the males in some species weighing up to five times as much as females. The four species that have been recorded along the California coast are Steller's sea lion, the California sea lion, the Guadalupe fur seal, and the northern fur seal.

Steller's sea lion (*Eumetopias jubata*)

Total length, males a maximum of 10 feet, 6 inches, females up to 7 feet, 6 inches; weight, males reaching 2,200 pounds, females 600 pounds; light yellowish but varying from almost cream color to yellowish brown; flippers blackish.

Steller's sea lion, also known as the northern sea lion, occurs around the margin of the North Pacific Ocean from Hokkaido and the Kurile Islands to the Santa Barbara Channel Islands of California. It ranges north of the Aleutian Islands in Bering Sea to the Pribilof Islands and in summer to St. Lawrence Island.

Unlike the California sea lion, Steller's sea lion does not habitually enter bays, estuaries, or river mouths. It is a species of the outer coast, hauling out on rugged offshore rocks. A few breed presently on San Miguel, the most northern of the Santa Barbara Channel Islands, but the most important breeding rookery is on Año Nuevo Island off the coast of southern San Mateo County. Prior to the beginning of the twentieth century there was a breeding colony on Seal Rocks in San Francisco County, and remains of skulls of pups found in piles of bones left by the early sealers on the Farallon Islands indicate that the species probably bred there,

[46]

too. Commercial exploitation in the nineteenth century, however, exterminated these breeding populations. The Año Nuevo colony, though heavily preyed upon by sealers, survived and presently during the summer more than 2,000 adults may be there.

The social behavior of Steller's sea lion in some respects resembles that of the northern fur seal, although there are many differences between the two species. On Año Nuevo Island the adult males begin arriving in early May, with maximum numbers present by late June or early July. They start leaving the island in late July and essentially all are gone by the beginning of September. The dominant bulls that will become harem masters begin establishing territories on the seaward reefs almost as soon as they arrive. They engage in considerable aggressive behavior and fierce battles take place. Only the most powerful and dominant individuals secure the most favorable positions. Defeated bulls remain on the periphery or in nonharem areas. Subadult males or bachelors gather in less favorable situations. Here they may engage in a sort of mock battle with one another.

Adult bulls when fighting face each other and lunge at the head and neck of the opponent. Their powerful teeth and jaws can do great damage and most harem bulls show numerous scars of battle. Defeated bulls may have many open wounds on head and neck. When defending territory the bulls roar, with a sound quite different from the staccato bark of the California sea lion. This roar combined with the comparatively long, manelike hair on the neck may account for the name "sea lion."

Although some females, or cows, are present on Año Nuevo Island all year, a great influx occurs in late May and June with peak numbers in July and August. Harems begin to form in late May and a single male may acquire as many as thirty cows, although the number is usually much smaller. While bulls try to keep cows from straying out of their own territories, which may

[47]

be no more than 20 feet in diameter, they do not herd them forcefully as does the northern fur seal bull.

The females bear their single young any time from about June 1 to July 15. The fur of the pups is a dark, grizzled brownish gray, which looks almost black when wet. Their calls remind one of the bleat of a lamb, and these vocal utterances seem to be important in assisting females to locate their young. During the first week or two after birth there is fairly high mortality among the young. Some of the pups are crushed by the harem bulls, who pay no attention to them, and some are swept off the reefs by rough seas. The young can swim but often are unable to get back up on the reefs, or else they swim away and become lost. When they are several weeks old they tend to sleep in groups on the edge of the harem areas where it is safer. Much of their waking time is spent swimming in the tidepools. By the time they are about two and a half months old they spend much of the day in surge channels and swim between the rookery reefs. The young nurse for many months, and it is not uncommon to see females with yearling young and tiny pups both nursing.

The bulls and bachelors are believed to move northward when they leave the rookery area in late summer. During the fall and winter aggregations of Steller's sea lions may be seen on offshore rocks at certain places along the northern California coast, but the number of individuals is not great. By late fall or early winter many of the females and young also leave the rookeries, and by January the local population reaches its minimum.

California sea lion *(Zalophus californianus)*

Total length, males up to 8 feet, females about 6 feet; weight, males up to 600 pounds, females about 200 pounds; general color, dark brown, although females are usually considerably lighter than males; adult males with a prominent crest on the head, hair of the crest lighter than on the rest of the body.

The California sea lion is a species of temperate to subtropical waters. It is known to breed on offshore islands along the Pacific Coast of North America from the Santa Barbara Channel Islands south to the San Benito Islands off the west coast of Baja California, on some islands in the Gulf of California, and along the west coast of the mainland of Mexico south probably to Mazatlán. Within historic times it has also been known to occur on the Tres Marías Islands. Post-breeding movements, primarily by adult and subadult males, extend northward to British Columbia. Another subspecific population (*Zalophus californianus wollebaeki*) is present in the Galápagos Islands on the equator, and a third subspecies (*Z. c. japonicus*), probably now extinct, occurred off the coast of Japan.

California sea lions are common zoo and circus animals. They train easily and do well in captivity. They are the most abundant and most commonly seen pinnipeds along the California coast. Their smaller size, dark coloration, and staccato, barklike calls readily distinguish them from Steller's sea lions with which they are often associated. In the water they are quite curious and often come close to fishing boats, if unmolested, and like to investigate the activities of skin and scuba divers. They are rapid and skillful swimmers, making use of the large front flippers for propulsion. At times when trying to make speed they "porpoise" on the surface and leap out of the water. They also seem to enjoy riding the waves as a surfer does. Individuals spend much time resting on sandy beaches or flat reefs of offshore islands, though they may also haul out on rather inaccessible beaches along the mainland, where they can be seen by observers but not easily bothered. Such areas are to be found along the Monterey coast and on Point Reyes in Marin County. Groups of individuals may rest on the surface of the water in rafts both during the day and at night. At such times a flipper is often raised into the air.

The breeding season for the California sea lion along the California coast is June and July. Just prior to this the males, which for much of the year stay north of the area occupied by the females and immatures, move south to the rookery beaches and reefs of the Santa Barbara Channel Islands and to islands farther south. The bulls become strongly territorial and aggressive and those that are dominant establish harem areas. These are adjacent to water and may be patrolled largely in the water by the bulls. Defense consists of nearly constant barking, threatening movements toward intruding bulls and, frequently, violent fighting. Territories may be held for as much as two weeks, which is a much shorter time than those held by northern fur seal bulls.

Females are gregarious at all seasons of the year. They do not necessarily stay with the same bull for any length of time. A single male may have as many as fourteen females at a time. The females have a single young, usually born between the middle of June and the middle of July. About two weeks after the young is born the female is bred. Females tend their young carefully for the first few days following birth, but the pups grow rapidly and within several weeks tend to gather in aggregations much like Steller's sea lion pups. The females continue to nurse for many months and may do so for a year. During the early weeks of life the pups play in shallow water and on the land, but as they grow older they venture farther out to sea.

By late July and August the male exodus from the rookeries is underway and by late August and early September they can be seen in numbers along the northern California coast. More than 13,000 individuals were counted by the writer on Año Nuevo Island on August 30, 1963. They mingle with Steller's sea lions and elephant seals indiscriminately, with little antagonism exhibited by any of the species. It is not uncommon to observe California sea lions sleeping on top of elephant seals in areas where the two species occur in numbers.

The enemies of this species, as with most pinnipeds, probably include large predatory sharks, killer whales, and man.

Guadalupe fur seal *(Arctocephalus townsendi)*

Total length, males approximately 6 feet, females considerably smaller; weight, males about 300 pounds, females' weight not recorded but probably less than 100 pounds; muzzle proportionately long and pointed; forehead rising rather abruptly; flippers proportionately long; general color of fur a rich chestnut, with whitish tips to the coarser hairs producing a somewhat grayish or grizzled effect.

The present population of Guadalupe fur seals, numbering about 500 individuals, is almost entirely confined to the Guadalupe Island area off the west coast of Baja California, although there have been a few sightings in recent years on San Miguel and San Nicolas islands off southern California. This species was believed to have been common in the early days of sealing as far north as the Farallon Islands. Between 1810 and 1812, according to records, 73,402 skins of fur seals were taken at the Farallons. Although the sealers did not distinguish between the northern fur seal *(Callorhinus ursinus)* and the more southern species, the animals were taken at a time of year when, according to later investigators, northern fur seals would have been absent or scarce. It was presumed, therefore, that most of those taken were of the Guadalupe type. The recent establishment of a northern fur seal colony on San Miguel Island casts some doubt on this theory.

The pointed muzzle, absence of a conspicuous crest on the head, proportionately long front and hind flippers, and thick, grizzled fur are characters that combine to separate this species from any other pinnipeds along the Pacific Coast of North America. Although some experts are inclined to regard the Guadalupe fur seal as identical with the South American fur seal (*Arcto-cephalus philippi*), it seems best to consider it as a separate species until more is known about its relation to other members of the genus which are of southern hemispheric distribution.

The little information available on the habits of the Guadalupe fur seals shows that at present they tend to spend much time in sea caves where they are difficult to observe. This habit may have been a factor responsible for the survival of a small population in spite of the inroads of the early fur sealers.

The bulls secure territories in or near sea caves and acquire harems of females numbering around ten individuals. The young are born in May, June, and July and after several weeks spend much time playing in tidepools. The common call of the males is described as a "bark," but it differs from that of California sea lions or northern fur seals. They may also utter a high-pitched "roar" when disturbed—even the young do this —but the sound is described as different from the calls of any other northern members of the family Otariidae.

The rediscovery in the early 1950s of this species, thought to be extinct, and the subsequent slow but constant increase in its numbers provide hope that the Guadalupe fur seal may come back as a significant member of California's marine mammal fauna.

Northern fur seal *(Callorhinus ursinus)*

Total length, males about 7 feet, females nearly 5 feet; weight, males 400 to 600 pounds, females 95 to 110 pounds; nose pointed but muzzle short; profile of head decidedly convex from nose to neck; adult males dark brown with neck and shoulders somewhat grizzled; adult females dark gray above, lighter beneath; hind flippers proportionately very long.

Although few persons see northern fur seals from shore in California, they are common off the coast in winter. The important part they played in the early history of exploration of the Pacific Coast justifies a rather thorough account.

The first European scientist to observe this species was Georg Wilhelm Steller, who accompanied Vitus Bering in his search for Alaska. On August 10, 1741, he sighted what are believed to have been fur seals. Steller again observed the species the following summer on Bering Island, where he was shipwrecked. In 1751 he published a description of this animal, and it was given its scientific name in 1758 by the great Swedish naturalist Linnaeus.

During succeeding years the northern fur seal, sometimes called the Alaska or Pribilof fur seal, became well known to sealers. Millions of these animals were slaughtered for their fur, which is fine and thick, unlike that of sea lions. Sealing was carried on not only on the principal rookery islands, which are the Pribilof and Commander islands in the Bering Sea, but on the open ocean, where the seals spend much of the year, south to the coast of California. It is said that the Russians took more than two and a half million fur seal pelts on the Pribilof Islands between the time Pribilof discovered the breeding rookeries in 1786 and the purchase of Alaska by the United States from Russia in 1867. Subsequently legislation was enacted which set the islands aside as a reservation for the northern fur seals and regulations were established governing the taking of these animals there. Unrestricted sealing, however, continued on the high seas and, since the majority of the fur seals taken by pelagic sealers were pregnant females or females with dependent pups on shore, and a great many of those shot were lost, the effect on the herd was serious. A multilateral convention was finally concluded in 1911 among Great Britain, Japan, Russia, and the United States prohibiting pelagic sealing, except by aborigines, and regulating the harvest on the rookery islands. The treaty was terminated by Japan in 1941 but in 1957 a new convention was signed, similar to that of 1911, by Canada, Japan, the Union of Soviet

Socialist Republics, and the United States. Presently the northern fur seal population has increased to more than one and a half million, permitting a selective harvest of over 60,000 individuals annually.

Because of the economic value of the northern fur seal and the intensive studies that have been made of it by biologists, more is known about its habits and movements than about any other pinniped. Until the summer of 1968 the known breeding rookeries were the Pribilof Islands of Alaska, the Commander Islands off Kamchatka, Robben Island off Sakhalin, and some of the Kurile Islands. In June 1968, however, a group of about 100 individuals was observed on the shore of San Miguel Island off southern California. Forty of these were newborn pups, sixty were females, and one was a bull. Several harems were found there in 1969 and again in 1970. The island is several thousand miles south of the previously known breeding range, and the presence of fur seals there may be an indication that the species, prior to its decimation by man, had a range not unlike that of Steller's sea lion. The San Miguel Island population is being carefully watched, but little is known as yet of the seasonal movements of the individuals comprising it except that bands found on four of the females were attached by the U.S. Government on St. Paul Island and one by the U.S.S.R. on Bering Island of the Commander group.

The northern fur seal is a social animal, but unlike most pinnipeds it generally comes to land only during the reproductive season. The adult males winter principally in the Gulf of Alaska, while the females and immatures move southward along the Pacific Coast of North America as far as the Santa Barbara Channel Islands of California and along the Asiatic coast to Japan. They are most abundant thirty to seventy miles offshore.

In late April the bulls begin to move northward. On the Pribilof Islands, where about 80 percent of the northern fur seals breed, they increase in numbers until mid-June. The older and more dominant bulls are the first to arrive at the rookery areas and by aggressive behavior establish their territories, which they hold unless vanquished by another bull. The females do not appear until June, when the bulls with the most favorable territory acquire the largest harems. Some bulls may win as many as a hundred cows while others have only one, the average being around forty. Most of the females have their young during the first three weeks of July and are bred five days after giving birth. A female will remain with her pup for about a week, following which she will regularly go to sea to feed. Such excursions last about eight days. During her absence the young survives on the rich milk it has consumed. The bulls do not leave the rookery from the time they arrive until the harems break up in late July or early August. The immature or subadult males are not allowed in the harem areas and gather apart in bachelor groups upon their arrival between June and early August. Nursing continues until late fall when the females leave and the young are on their own. They leave the islands by November and go to sea. A few return the following autumn for a short time, but the majority do not come back until the second or third year of life.

EARLESS SEALS
Family Phocidae

The earless seals are often known as hair seals. The term "earless" refers to the absence of an external pinna which, though small, is present in all members of the Otariidae. The hind flippers of the earless seals cannot be brought under the body and used for locomotion on land. The nails are developed equally on all five digits. The front flippers are relatively small with well-developed claws and play an insignificant role in propulsion, which is accomplished by lateral, fishlike movement of the posterior part of the body.

The earless seals are more widely distributed, especially in the Arctic and Antarctic, than the eared seals. Of the thirteen living genera, including eighteen species, two occur along the California coast—the harbor seal and the northern elephant seal.

Harbor seal *(Phoca vitulina)*

Total length, males 5 to nearly 6 feet, females 4 to 5 feet; weight, males up to about 250 pounds, females somewhat less; muzzle short and head noticeably round; color extremely variable, ranging from a pale silver gray spotted with black to dark brown or almost black with spots hardly discernible; flippers well haired.

The harbor seal, or common seal as it is called in Europe, has a very extensive range. It occurs along parts of the arctic coasts of North America, Europe, and Asia as well as southward along the coasts of all three continents. Along the east coast of North America harbor seals have been recorded south to North Carolina. They are known to occur along the European coast south to Portugal and in the Baltic Sea. In the western Pacific harbor seals range south to the coast of China and in the eastern Pacific south to the west coast of Baja California.

Harbor seals are fairly common along the coast of California but are never found in large numbers. They usually occur in groups ranging from a few individuals to as many as a hundred but do not exhibit the sort of social behavior that is so characteristic of sea lions, fur seals, and elephant seals. Harbor seals often come into bays and estuaries and may be seen resting on sand bars at low tide. Along the outer coast they also tend to haul out on reefs or small offshore rocks at low tide. On islands they are frequently seen lying on rocky ledges in the late afternoon. Members of this species are very wary and are able to detect the approach of a human being from a considerable distance. They seldom venture far from the water, in which they take refuge at the first intimation of danger. Their movements on land are clumsy, effected by sort of hopping on their bellies like inch worms.

In the water harbor seals often move with their round heads above the surface so they can observe. They are quite curious and may follow a person, staying 50 to 100 yards offshore as one walks along a beach or a cliff above the sea.

Members of this species are notably silent in contrast to many other pinnipeds. Frequently they slap the surface of the water with their flippers, producing a loud noise which can be heard for some distance, resembling the sound made by a beaver slapping the water with its tail to signal danger.

Along the California coast females have their young between March and early May. The young are usually born at low tide on a reef or sandbar and are able to swim very shortly thereafter, staying rather close to the mother. They weigh about 25 pounds at birth and are weaned in about three weeks. They are very light in color, sometimes born with an embryonic coat of soft, whitish hair which is soon lost.

It is not uncommon for persons to find newborn harbor seals on beaches or reefs and bring them to local museums or aquariums in the belief that they have been abandoned. In most instances they were probably not abandoned, and the mother was undoubtedly not far from shore, watching anxiously as her offspring was removed.

We know little of the reproductive behavior of this species though it appears that mating takes place in the water. The males do not have territories or acquire harems of females as in social species of pinnipeds.

The food of harbor seals consists largely of fishes found along shore and in bays and estuaries.

Northern elephant seal *(Mirounga angustirostris)*

Total length, males reportedly up to over 20 feet, females up to 11 feet, 5 inches; weight, males estimated up to 8,000 pounds, females up to 2,000 pounds; adult males with inflatable proboscis, absent in females; general color of adult males in fresh pelage, dark gray above, lighter below, with thick, furrowed skin of exposed neck pinkish gray; general color of males in worn pelage, dark brown; females generally browner and darker than males; newborn young blackish; immatures silvery gray to pale, yellowish gray.

There are two rather closely related species of elephant seals living today. One of these, the southern elephant seal *(Mirounga leonina)*, is circumpolar in the southern hemisphere and primarily associated with subantarctic islands. The northern elephant seal is separated from its southern relative by many thousands of miles and has a much more restricted distribution. According to early reports such as those of Captain Scammon, it formerly occurred from Cabo San Lázaro on the west coast of Baja California north to Point Reyes, Marin County, California. The species was nearly exterminated, however, by the middle of the nineteenth century as a result of commercial sealing for oil and hides. A small nucleus of a population did survive on Guadalupe Island off the coast of Baja California, and at the beginning of the twentieth century it was estimated to number about a hundred individuals.

With protection the northern elephant seal has gradually come back and now may be found regularly on a number of Pacific Coast islands, including the San Benitos, San Geronimo, Guadalupe, and Los Coronados in Baja California, and San Nicolas, San Miguel, Año Nuevo, and the Farallons in California waters. The largest concentration is on Guadalupe, where more than 15,000 individuals have been recorded at one time. Most recently a breeding rookery has been established on Año Nuevo, where young have been born every winter since 1960–1961. Some elephant seals haul out on the Farallon Islands but to date no reproduction has been observed there.

The northern elephant seal is a social pinniped, but

its social behavior differs in a number of respects from that of fur seals and sea lions whose dominant males, during the breeding season, defend their harem territories. There is no territorial defense of this sort by male elephant seals but rather a social hierarchy, or peck order, in which the most aggressive and dominant males mate with the greatest number of females. Studies made on Año Nuevo indicate that 4 percent of the adult males inseminate 85 percent of the females.

Breeding activity in the northern elephant seal is restricted to the winter months. On most islands sandy or rocky beaches are selected for this purpose, rather than reefs. The adult males arrive at Año Nuevo Island, and probably at all the other island rookeries, in December, and most of them remain until March. Several weeks after the arrival of the bulls the females begin to make their appearance and shortly thereafter give birth to a single young. The first young are born by the beginning of January.

The dominant bulls exhibit aggressive behavior by raising their heads and necks high in the air at the approach of another male elephant seal and uttering a series of low-pitched grunts, with the mouth open and the long, pendulous proboscis hanging into it. If this does not deter the intruding male there may be physical encounter with the two animals facing one another, each trying to bite and push his opponent. After a few seconds one of the two will retreat. Since land territories are not maintained, the most dominant bull in a rookery will occupy the area in which the most females are located. This may shift from place to place with the movement of the females. The latter regularly go into the water, possibly to feed, and return to their young. The young nurse for about three or four weeks, more than quadrupling their weight. Then the females are bred and soon leave the rookeries.

The males completely disregard the young and, in moving about, crush many with their enormous weight. During the breeding season the bulls are aggressive toward human intruders and will lumber toward an approaching person with head raised and mouth open. The females will sometimes open their mouths and call if a person approaches them. For the most part, during the nonreproductive season elephant seals pay little attention to man. They are easy to approach, and if they are asleep one can walk among them.

When the adult males and females depart from the rookeries in March, the young of the year are left behind, and they stay on the beach until the latter part of May. During this time they increase in length and decrease in diameter. When about one month old they lose the very dark, almost black, and somewhat curly natal pelage and acquire a silver gray coat composed of shorter hairs. No food is eaten during this period on the beach.

Correlated with the departure of the adults from the rookery beaches is the arrival of immature animals, probably one to several years of age. This results in a population peak in the spring. By late May many of these immatures, along with the young of the year, leave and adult and subadult males come to shore to undergo a molt during the summer. The adults and subadults leave by the end of summer and another influx of immatures occurs.

Little is known as yet about where elephant seals go when they leave the rookery areas. Banding, however, has shown that young of the year born on islands off the coast of Baja California may move north to central California when only a few months old. It is suspected that the adults and subadults spend much of the year at sea, not in groups but singly.

SUGGESTED REFERENCES

Bartholomew, G. A., Jr. Reproductive and social behavior of the northern elephant seal. University of
California Publications in Zoology, 47 (1952): 369–
429, pls. 38–57.

Brownell, R. L., Jr. Observations of odontocetes in central California waters. Norsk Hvalfangst-Tidende
no. 3, 1964, pp. 60–66.

Daugherty, A. E. Marine mammals of California. California Department of Fish and Game, Sacramento,
1965. 87 pp.

Gaskin, D. E. The New Zealand Cetacea. Fisheries Research Bulletin no. 1 (new series), New Zealand
Marine Department, 1968. 92 pp.

Gilmore, R. M. 1958. The story of the gray whale. Pri-
vately published, San Diego, Calif. 16 pp.

Grinnell, J., J. S. Dixon, and J. M. Linsdale. Fur-bearing
mammals of California, vol. 1. Berkeley: University
of California Press, 1937. 375 pp.

Harrison, R. J., and J. E. King. Marine mammals. London: Hutchinson University Library, 1965. 192 pp.

Kenyon, K. W. The sea otter in the eastern Pacific
Ocean. United States Bureau of Sport Fisheries and
Wildlife, North American Fauna, no. 68, 1969. 352
pp.

King, J. E. Seals of the world. London: British Museum
(Natural History), 1964. 154 pp.

LeBoeuf, B. J., and R. S. Peterson. Social status and
mating activity in elephant seals. Science, 163 (1969):
91–93.

Nishiwaki, M. Distribution and migration of marine
mammals in the North Pacific area. Tokyo: Ocean
Research Institute, University of Tokyo, 1966. 49 pp.

Norris, K. S., editor. Whales, porpoises, and dolphins.
Berkeley and Los Angeles: University of California
Press, 1966. 789 pp.

[61]

Ogden, A. The California sea otter trade, 1784–1848. Berkeley and Los Angeles: University of California Press, 1941. 251 pp.

Orr, R. T., and T. C. Poulter. Año Nuevo Marine Biological Park. Pacific Discovery, 15 (1962), no. 1:13-19.

Orr, R. T., and T. C. Poulter. The pinniped population of Año Nuevo Island. Proceedings of the California Academy of Sciences, ser. 4, 32 (1965): 377–404.

Orr, R. T., and T. C. Poulter. Some observations on reproduction, growth, and social behavior in the Steller sea lion. Proceedings of the California Academy of Sciences, ser. 4, 35 (1967): 193–226.

Peterson, R. S., and G. A. Bartholomew. The natural history and behavior of the California sea lion. American Society of Mammalogists, Special Publication No. 1, 1967. 79 pp.

Pike, G. C. Guide to the whales, porpoises and dolphins of the north-east Pacific and arctic waters of Canada and Alaska. Nanaimo, B.C.: Fisheries Research Board of Canada, Circular No. 32, 1956. 14 pp.

Radford, K. W., R. T. Orr, and C. Hubbs. Reestablishment of the northern elephant seal (*Mirounga angustirostris*) off central California. Proceedings of the California Academy of Sciences, ser. 4, 31 (1965): 601–612.

Rice, D. W. Cetaceans, pp. 291–324. *In*: S. Anderson and J. K. Jones, Jr., Recent mammals of the world; a synopsis of families. New York: Ronald Press, 1967.

Rice, D. W., and A. A. Wolman. The life history and ecology of the gray whale (*Eschrichtius robustus*). American Society of Mammalogists, Special Publication No. 3, 1971. 142 pp.

Scheffer, V. B. Seals, sea lions, and walruses; a review of the Pinnipedia. Stanford: Stanford University Press, 1958. 179 pp.

Slijper, E. J. Whales. New York: Basic Books, Inc., 1962. 475 pp.

Walker, T. J. Whale primer. San Diego: Cabrillo Historical Association, 1962. 58 pp.

INDEX